Looking at Life Cycles

Oak Tree

Victoria Huseby

A⁺

Smart Apple Media

Smart Apple Media is published by Black Rabbit Books
P.O. Box 3263, Mankato, Minnesota 56002

Printed in the United States

Published by arrangement with the Watts Publishing Group Ltd, London.

Editor: Rachel Tonkin
Designer: Proof Books
Picture researcher: Diana Morris
Literacy consultant: Gill Matthews
Science consultant: Andrew Solway

Picture credits:
Campbell/Topfoto: 15; Malcolm Forrow/Photographers Direct: 13;
Bob Gibbons/OSF: 4; Michael Gadomski/Photographers Direct: 9;
Duncan McEwan/NaturePL: 17, 19; Richard Packwood/OSF: front cover: 1, 21;
Gary K. Smith/FLPA: 7; Superbild/AlPix: 11; Adrian Thomas/SPL: 5

Library of Congress Cataloging-in-Publication Data

Huseby, Victoria.
      Oak tree / by Victoria Huseby.
      p. cm.— (Smart Apple Media. Looking at life cycles)
      Summary: "An introduction to the life cycle of an oak tree, including how it grows from acorn to
adult and how the tree makes new acorns"—Provided by publisher.
      Includes index.
      ISBN 978-1-59920-178-8
      1. Oak—Life cycles—Juvenile literature. I. Title.
QK495.F14H87 2009
583'.46—dc22
                                                                                              2007030465

9 8 7 6 5 4 3 2 1

Contents

Seed

An oak tree is a flowering
plant. It grows from a
seed called an acorn.
Acorns grow on an
oak tree every year.

5

Acorns Buried

In fall, acorns fall to the ground. Squirrels collect and bury some acorns to eat during winter. They forget where some of the acorns are, and these stay under the ground.

Root

Under the ground, the acorn begins to grow. A **root** grows out of the seed and down into the **soil**. The acorn contains a store of **energy** to help the root grow.

9

Shoot

A **shoot** then grows from
the acorn up through the
soil. The first leaves begin
to appear.

11

Seedling

The **seedling**'s leaves take
in energy from the sun.
This helps the seedling
grow bigger and bigger.

Young Tree

After about 20 years, the seedling grows into a young oak tree. The tree has many branches. Every fall, its leaves fall off. Every spring, the branches are covered in new leaves.

Catkins

When the oak tree is about 20 years old, it begins to produce **flowers** each spring. There are both male and female flowers. The male flowers are called **catkins**.

Acorns

Pollen from the catkins is blown by the wind onto the female flowers. The female flowers then become acorns.

Ancient Trees

The oak tree's cycle of new leaves, flowers, and acorns happens every year. Oak trees can live to be more than 1,000 years old.

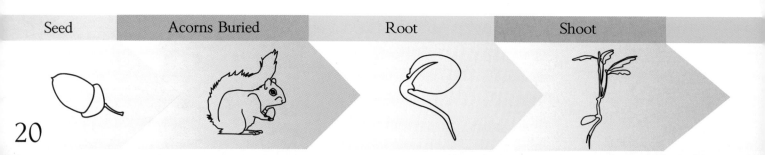

Seed   Acorns Buried   Root   Shoot

Seedling

Young Tree

Catkins

Ancient Trees

Oak Tree Facts

- Oak trees can grow to be more than 130 feet (40 m) high.

- An oak tree can take in more than 53 gallons (200 l) of water a day through its roots.

- Oak trees are more likely to be struck by lightning than any other tree.

- The oldest living oak tree is thought to be in Bulgaria in southeast Europe. The tree is about 1,650 years old.

- For every 10,000 acorns, only one will become an oak tree.

Glossary

Catkins
The fluffy flowers of an oak tree.

Energy
The strength or power to do things, such as grow.

Flowers
The colorful part of a plant in which the seed forms.

Pollen
A powder found in the flowers of plants. Pollen must move from one plant to another for seeds to form.

Root
The part of a plant that grows under the ground.

Seed
The part of a plant that grows to make a new plant.

Seedling
A young plant.

Shoot
The first growth of a young plant above the ground. Shoot also means any new growth, such as a bud or branch, from a plant.

Soil
The earth that plants grow in.

Index and Web Sites

For Kids:

BrainPOP Jr.: Plant Life Cycle
http://www.brainpopjr.com/science/
plants/plantlifecycle/

Trees
http://www.units.muohio.edu/
dragonfly/trees.htmlx

For Teachers:

**National Teacher Training Institute—
This Is Tree-rific!**
http://www.myetv.org/education/ntti/
lessons/2004_lessons/trees.cfm

Teacher's Domain: Plant Life Cycles
http://www.teachersdomain.org/
resources/tdc02/sci/life/colt/
lp_plantcycle/index.html